HURRY
HURRY

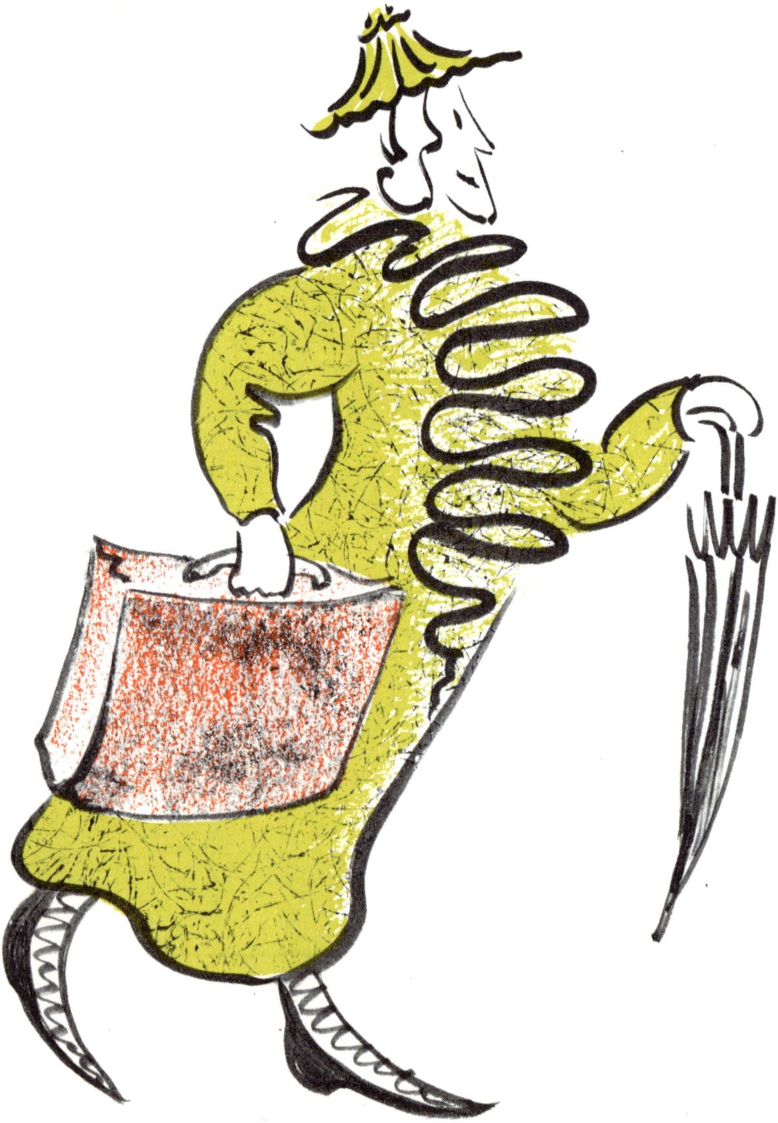

HURRY HURRY

An **I CAN READ** Book

by
EDITH THACHER HURD

Pictures by
CLEMENT HURD

HARPER & ROW, PUBLISHERS
NEW YORK AND EVANSTON

HURRY HURRY
Text copyright © 1960 by Edith Thacher Hurd
Pictures copyright © 1960 by Clement G. Hurd
Printed in the United States of America

All rights reserved. Printed in the United States of America. No part of this book may be used or reproduced in any manner whatsoever without written permission except in the case of brief quotations embodied in critical articles and reviews. For information address Harper & Row, Publishers, Inc., 10 East 53rd Street, New York, N.Y. 10022.

This book is based on a story with the same title first published in 1938.

Library of Congress catalog card number: 60-9453

HURRY
HURRY

"Good-bye, good-bye," said Suzie.

"Good-bye, dear Mother. Good-bye, dear Father. Have a lovely time."

Suzie's mother
and Suzie's father
were going away
for a day
or two.

So Miss Mugs,

funny old Miss Mugs,

came to stay.

Old Miss Mugs

came to stay for a day

or two

with Suzie.

Miss Mugs was nice
and Suzie liked her
but she was always in a hurry.

In the morning Miss Mugs said,

"Hurry, hurry.

Get up, Suzie,

or you will be late for school."

"Hurry,

brush your teeth."

"Hurry,

eat your breakfast."

"Hurry,

put your hat and coat on

or you will be late for school."

Miss Mugs did not wait for Suzie.

But off she went to school.

She was in such a hurry

she did not see the milkman.

What a mess!

There was milk on the milkman's hat.

There was milk on the milkman's coat.

There was milk on his shoes.

But Miss Mugs was in such a hurry

she hardly stopped to say

"Excuse me" to the milkman.

"Don't be in such a hurry

or something worse may happen,"

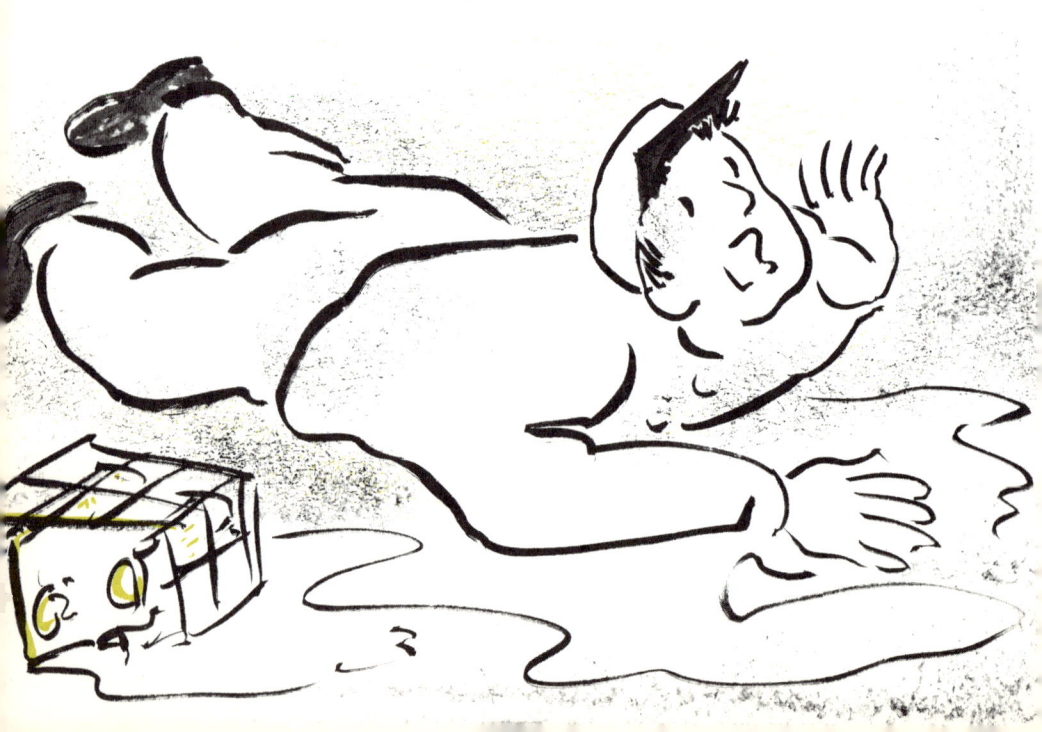

said the milkman.

"Yes," said Suzie.

"Don't be in such a hurry, Miss Mugs, or something worse may happen."

And it did.

It happened when Miss Mugs
did not see a fat lady
with three little cats and
one big dog.

What a mess!

But Miss Mugs was in such a hurry
she hardly stopped to say
"Excuse me."
"Look out," said the fat lady.
"Don't be in such a hurry.
Something worse may happen."
And it did.

It happened when Miss Mugs did not see a sign that said:

DANGER

Men at Work

Down she went.

Poor Miss Mugs.

Down in the hole.

Suzie heard her calling,

"Hurry, hurry.

Get me out of here

or Suzie will be late for school."

Suzie got the policeman
who got a rope
and pulled Miss Mugs out.

What a mess!

She had mud on her hat.

She had mud on her coat.

She had mud on her shoes.

But she did not stop to take the mud off.

She hardly stopped to say

"Thank you" to the policeman.

"Look out," said the policeman.
"Don't be in such a hurry
or something worse may happen."
And it did.

Miss Mugs was in such a hurry she did not see a steam shovel.

Up she went.

Poor Miss Mugs.

Up in the air.

"What are you doing up there?

Do you think you can fly

up there in the sky?"

said Suzie.

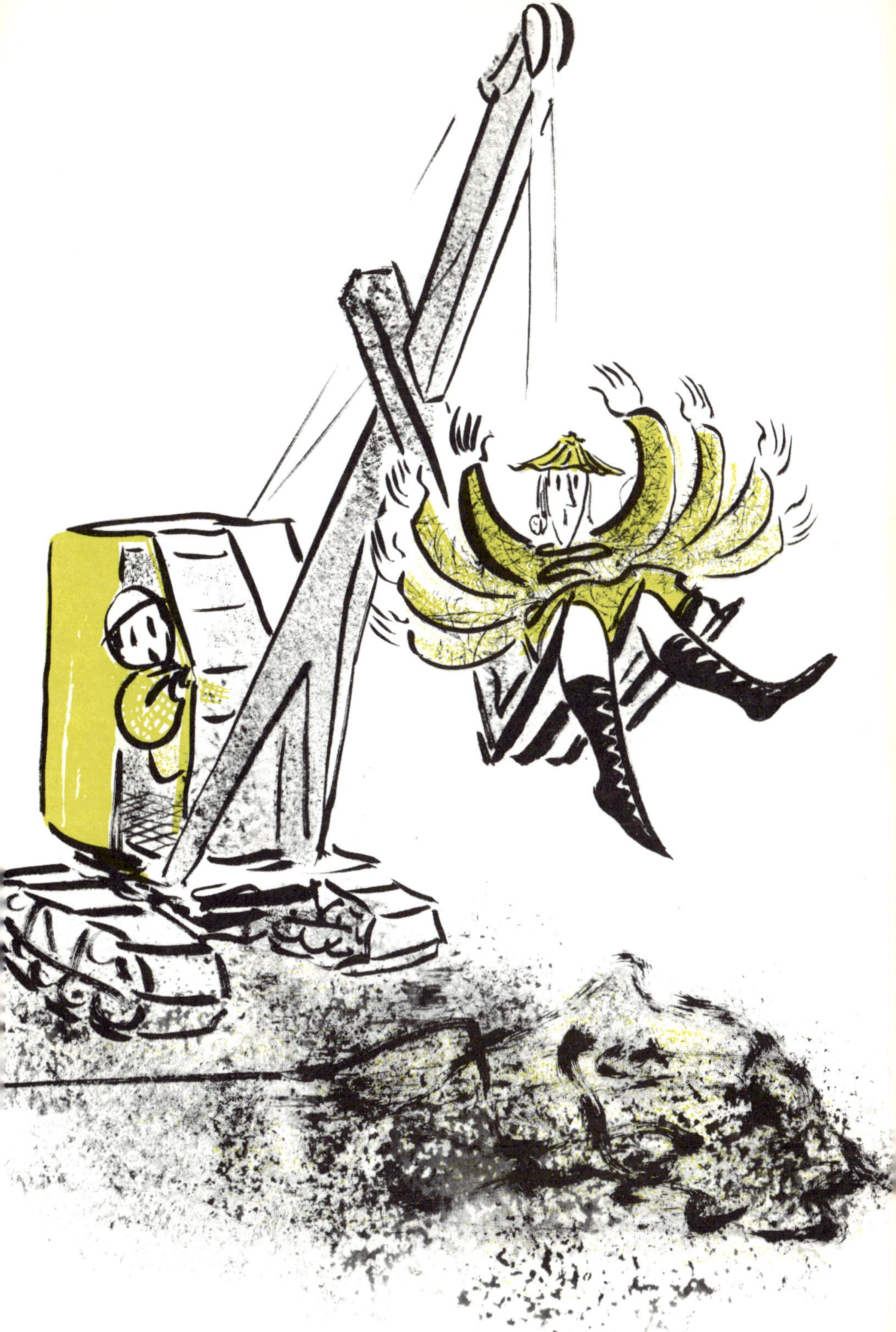

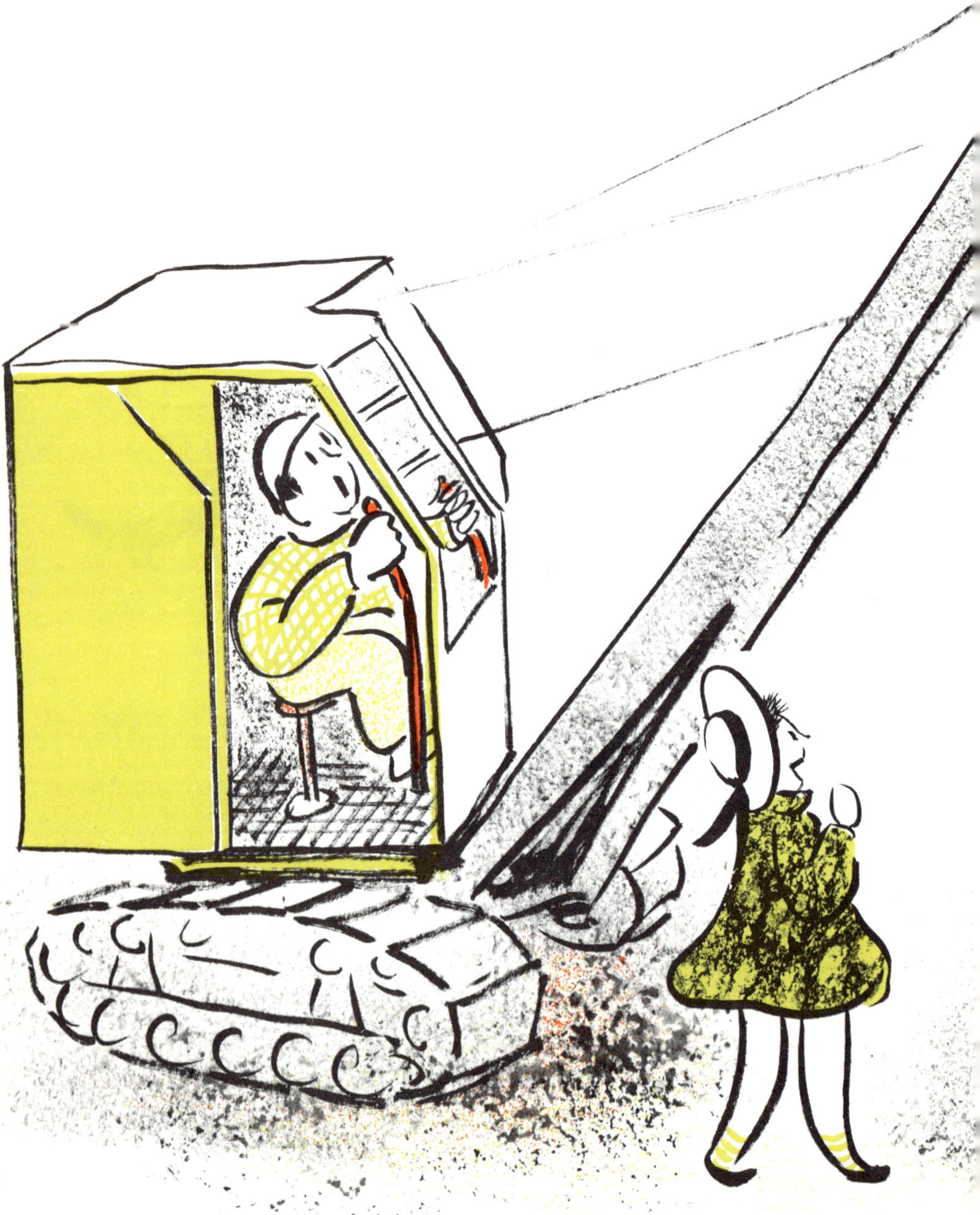

"Oh no," said poor Miss Mugs.
"Put me down. Put me down
or Suzie will be late for school."

So the man who ran the steam shovel
put Miss Mugs down.
"Look out," he said.
"Don't be in such a hurry
or something worse may happen."
And it did.

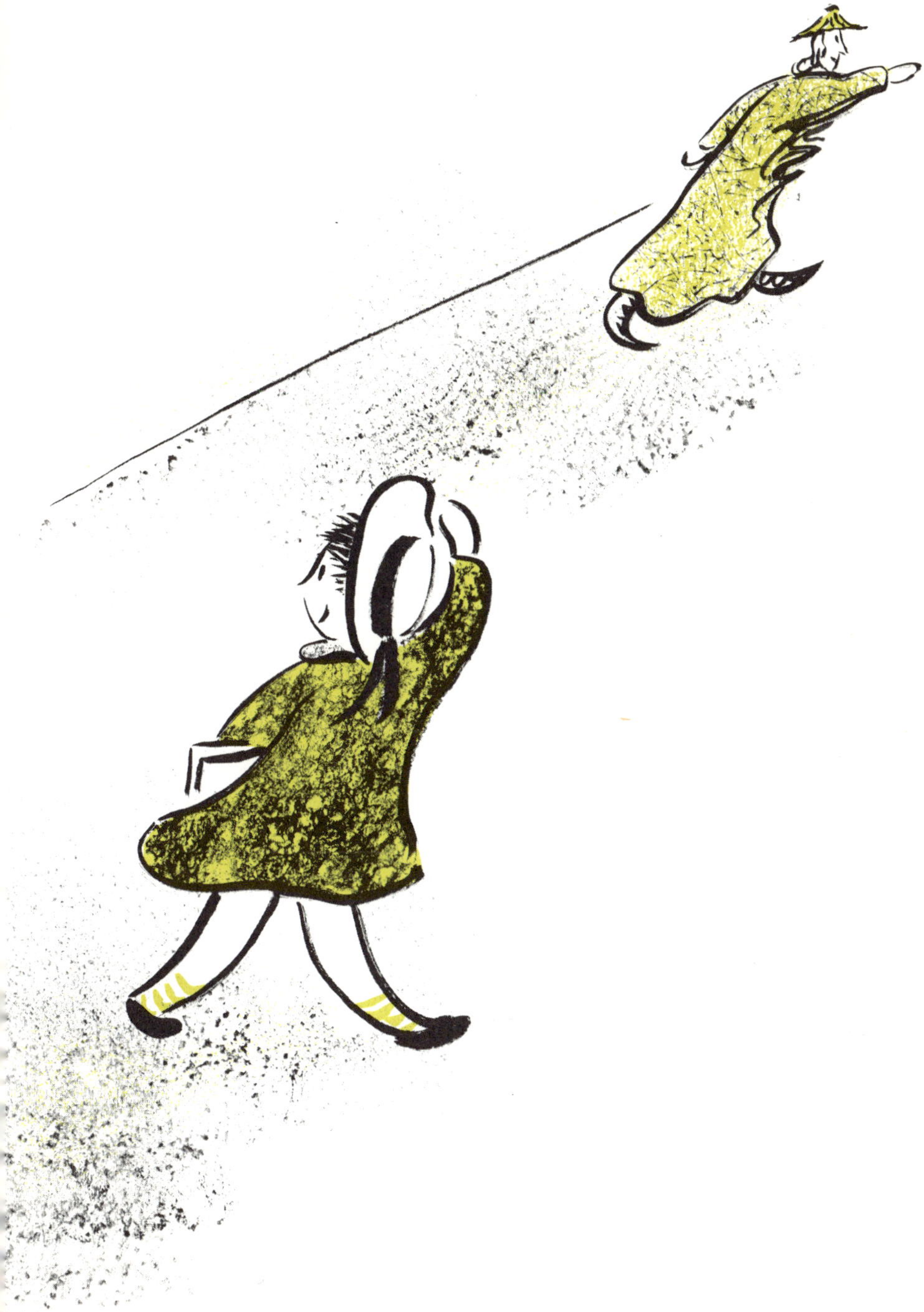

It happened when Miss Mugs
walked under a ladder.

"Look out," cried Suzie.

"Look out," cried the policeman.

But Miss Mugs was in too much of a hurry.

SO———

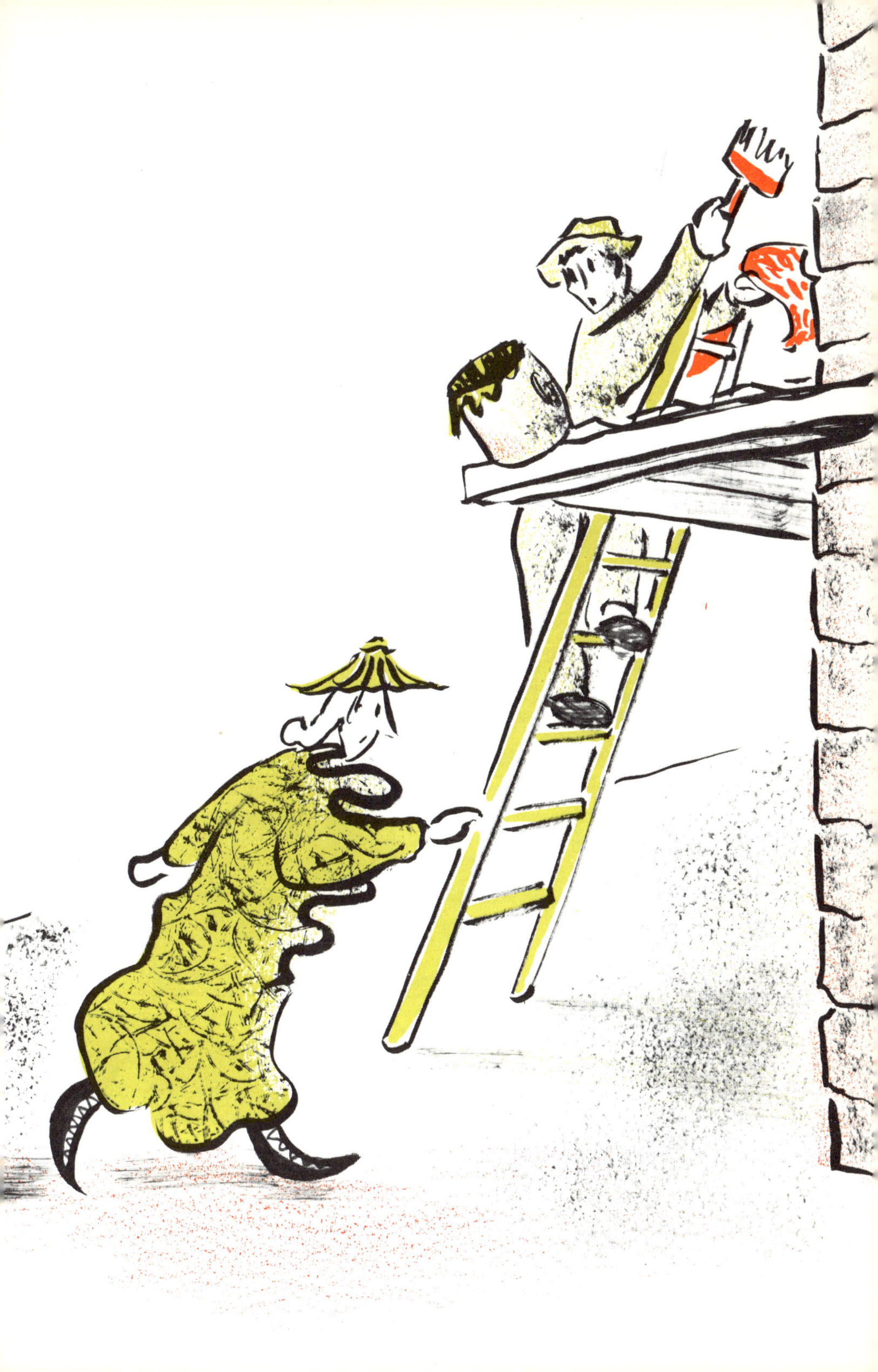

There she was

with a pot of glue over her head

AND THE GLUE RUNNING DOWN

ALL OVER HER!

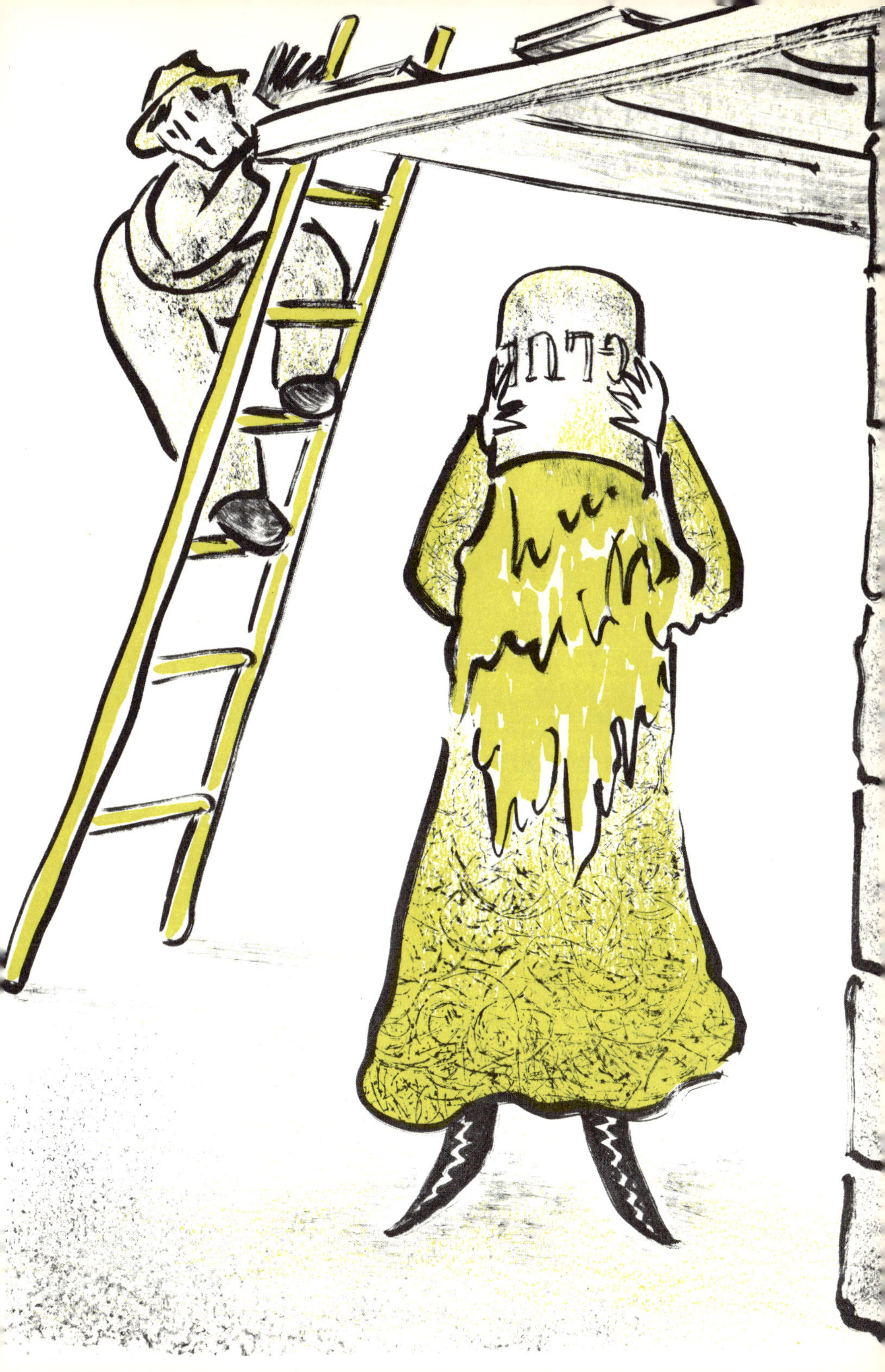

Suzie pulled.

The policeman pulled.

The milkman pulled.

The fat lady pulled.

Then they all pulled together
and the pot came off with a
GLUEY—GLUB!

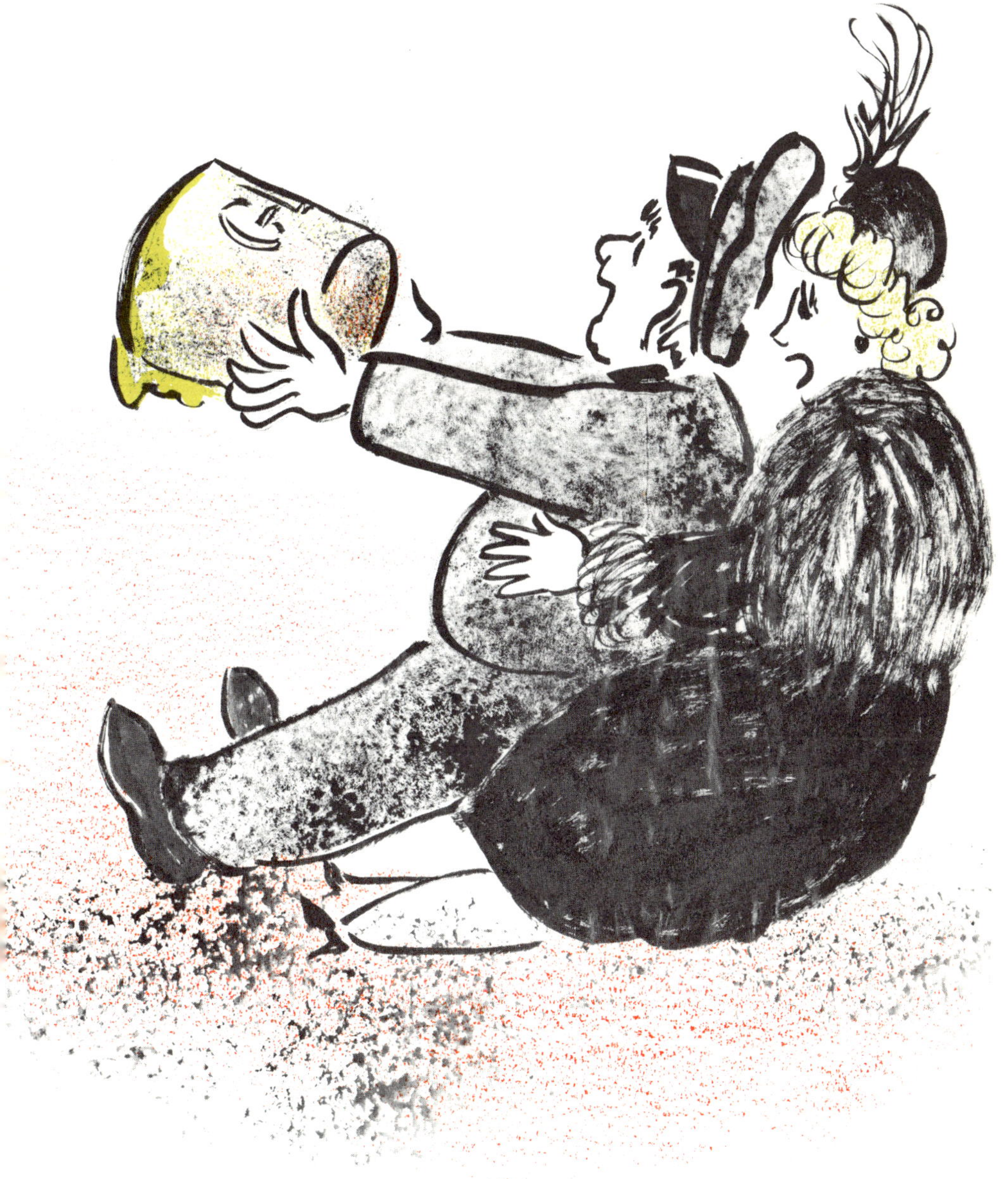

Miss Mugs was a mess.

She had glue on her hat.

She had glue on her coat.

She had glue on her shoes.

She couldn't move.

She couldn't walk.

But she could say—

"Hurry!

Get me out of this

or Suzie will be late for school."

"No," said Suzie.

"I will not get you out

if you say 'hurry' again."

"Oh, I won't," said Miss Mugs.

"I promise.

I won't say 'hurry' again

if you will get me out of this glue."

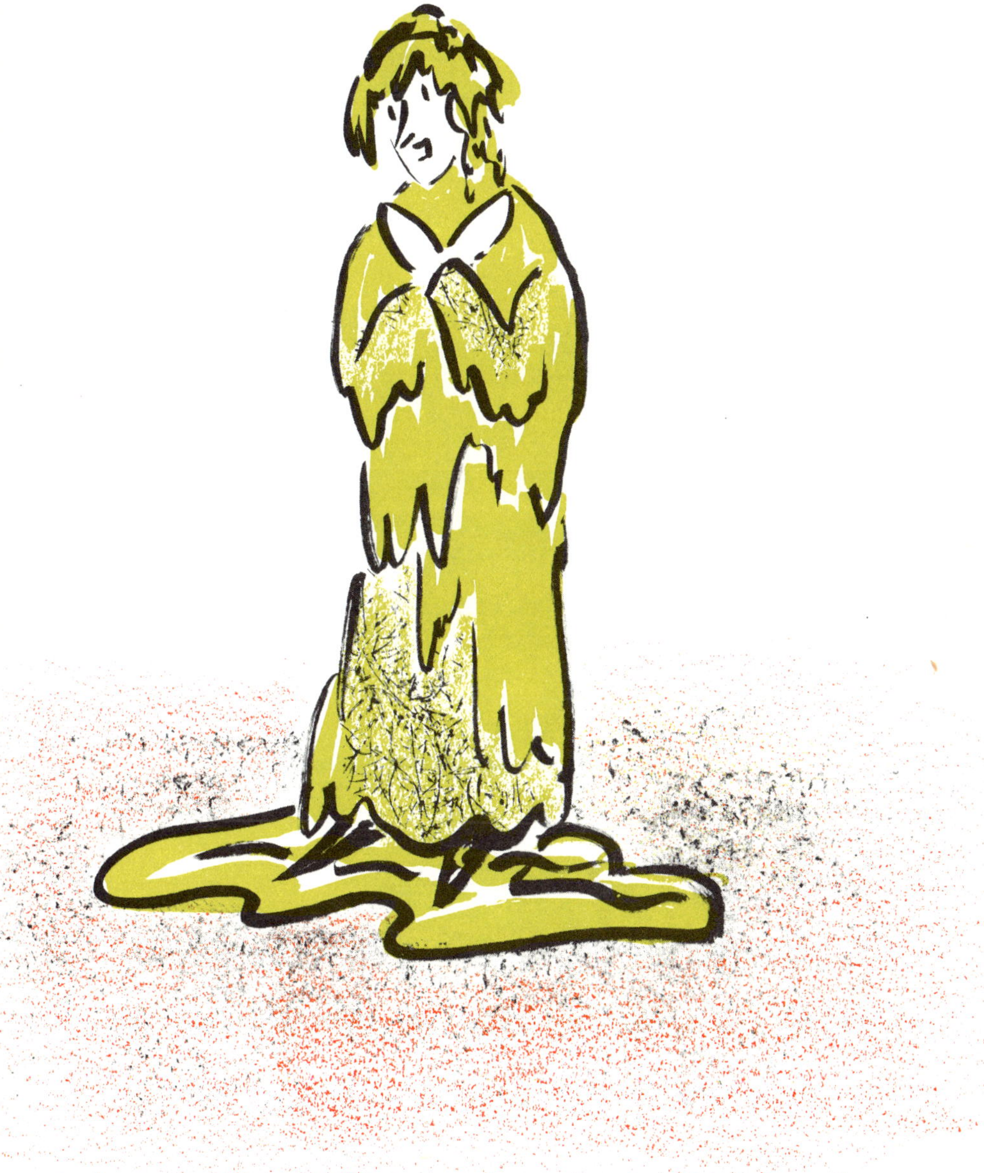

So Suzie scraped the glue
off Miss Mugs's hat.
She scraped the glue off
Miss Mugs's coat.
But when she got to her shoes
Miss Mugs said,
"Hurry!"

Suzie stopped.

"You promised not to say 'hurry.' But you did. So now I will not take the glue off your shoes."

Suzie started off to school.

"Oh no," said poor Miss Mugs.

"Suzie, Suzie, get me out of

this terrible glue.

I promise.

I promise I will never say 'hurry' again."

"Come on," said the policeman.
"We'd better get her out.
She's in everybody's way."
"She's always in MY way,"
said the milkman.

Suzie pulled.

The policeman pulled.

The milkman pulled.

Even the fat lady's dog pulled.

But they could not get Miss Mugs

out of the glue.

So they had to get the steam shovel
to come and SCOOP her out.

Miss Mugs almost said
"H — — —."
But then she said
"Thank you" instead.

There was still a little glue
on Miss Mugs's shoes
so she had to walk
very, very slowly.

One foot up—glub!

One foot down—glub!

Very, very slowly.

And the slower Miss Mugs walked the better she seemed to like it.

So when they got to school
and Suzie said she'd take
the glue off,

Miss Mugs smiled and said,

"I don't think I want you to.

For I've found out

it's fun to go slowly

and a terrible bother to hurry."

Then she walked home
very, very slowly!